at home with ...

The Victorians

...in history

KU-132-549

LLYFRGELLOEDD ABERTAWE
SWANSEA LIBRARIES

8000011527

WAYLAND

www.waylandbooks.co.uk

This paperback edition first published in Great Britain in 2017 by Wayland

Copyright © 2014 Brown Bear Books Ltd.

Wayland
An imprint of Hachette Children's Group
Part of Hodder & Stoughton
Carmelite House
50 Victoria Embankment
London EC4Y 0DZ
An Hachette UK Company
www.hachette.co.uk
www.hachettechildrens.co.uk

All Rights Reserved.

ISBN: 978 0 7502 8973 3

Brown Bear Books Ltd.
First Floor
9–17 St. Albans Place
London
N1 0NX

Author: Tim Cooke
Designer: Lynne Lennon
Picture manager: Sophie Mortimer
Design manager: Keith Davis
Editorial director: Lindsey Lowe
Children's publisher: Anne O'Daly

Printed in China

LLYFRGELLOEDD ABERTAWE SWANSEA LIBRARIES	
4000008126	
PETERS	£8.99
941.081	
SK	

Websites

The website addresses (URLs) included in this book were valid at the time of going to press. However, because of the nature of the internet, it is possible that some addresses may have changed, or sites may have changed or closed down since publication. While the author and publisher regret any inconvenience this may cause the readers, no responsibility for any such changes can be accepted by either the author or the publisher.

Picture credits

Key: b = bottom, bgr = background, c = centre, l = left, mtg = montage, r = right, t = top.

Front Cover: Library of Congress: l; **RHL: Woodysworld** main; **Shutterstock:** K. Jensen tr.
Interior : Alamy: Steven May 24bl, Wildlife GMBH 11cr; **fotoLibra:** 22; **istockphoto:** 16r; **Kobal Collection:** 20th Century Fos 27b; **Mary Evans Picture Library:** 7l, 21, Grenville Collins Postcard Collection 7br; **Library of Congress:** 4, 13t, 13b, 19b, 20, 23t, 29t, 29b; **RHL:** Bassano 5t, National Archives 18l; **Shutterstock:** 10, 14, 15, 23b, 24r, 26, 27c, 29bl, Accord 7t, Patrick Bombaert 14tr, Victoria Brassey 19cr, Joe Gough 17b, K. Jensen 27tr, Hodag Media 9br, J. Helgason 11b, Ed Isaacs 18r, Michael McDonal 25l, Richard Peterson 17t, D. Pimborough 16tr, Marco Jose Bastos Silva 12, Victorian Traditions 19l; **Snapshots of the Past:** 8t; **Thinkstock:** istockphoto 1, 5b, 9tl, 9-10b, Photos. com 6, 11t 23br, 25tr; **Topfoto:** Topham Picturepoint 28.

All other artworks Brown Bear Books.

Brown Bear Books has made every attempt to contact the copyright holder. If you have any information please contact licensing@brownbearbooks.co.uk

Contents

hello people! **Welcome to the Victorian World!** 4

our cities **Big City Slickers** 6

on the move **Getting Around** 8

my home **Our Homes are our Castles** 10

trip advisor **America Rules!** 12

style watch **Get the Look!** 14

master chef **Food and Drink** 16

makeover **Keeping Up Appearances** 18

which job? **You Can't Get the Staff** 20

time off **In Our Spare Time** 22

love to shop **We're All Consumers Now** 24

holiday time **Get in the Festive Spirit** 26

in the news **Read all About it!** 28

Glossary 30

On the Web / Books 31

Index 32

CROWDED slums, **mass** murderers
... No wonder we're the height of civilization!

Welcome to the Victorian World!

What do you know about the Victorians? Probably that they lived in big cities. That they travelled by railway. Maybe that they were very prudish (strict and proper). Correct?

Well, none of that is WRONG, but it's only PART of the story. We're going to take you behind the scenes.

Hot facts

★ **The Victorian** era coincided with the reign of Queen Victoria of Great Britain and Ireland from 1837 to 1901.

★ **Victoria** was also empress of the British Empire, which stretched around the world, from Australia and India to Canada.

★ **Victoria** married the German Prince Albert in 1840. After he died in 1861, she wore black mourning dress for the rest of her life.

★ **The Victorian age** was a time of great industrial and engineering progress, and also of social change.

＊ THE IRON WAY ＊
Railway tracks spread across Europe and North America. More than 18,000 miles were built in Britain alone!

THE AGE OF CHANGE

- Victoria's reign saw great changes in Europe and North America. More people lived in huge cities, more children went to school and more workers laboured in factories.
- Millions of immigrants from Europe arrived in the United States trying to find a better life.
- Slavery was abolished in Britain (1833) and the United States (1863).
- Settlers moved into the Midwest and to the West Coast, by wagon train or by railway.
- On both sides of the Atlantic, many people lived in overcrowded cities, full of disease, crime and poverty.
- From the middle of the 19th century, reformers tried to make new laws to improve living conditions for ordinary people.

I'd love to have a DAY OFF!

✳ LONG LIVE THE QUEEN! ✳
Longest rule of any British monarch. The Victorian age lasted 63 years and 7 months!

THE BRITISH EMPIRE 1914
British Possessions
Railways

World Empire
The British had colonies around the world. The most important were Canada, Australia and – above all – India. Because the colonies were all over the globe, they became known as 'the empire on which the sun never set'.

City SLICKERS

We Victorians are more likely to live in cities than people did in the past, especially in Europe. But although city life can be fun, it can have its problems, too.

Population

In Britain, just 20 percent of people lived in towns when Victoria became queen in 1837. In 1901, at the end of her reign, it's up to 75 per cent of Britons living in the rapidly expanding cities.

Keep on MOVING!

London is grinding to a halt. But we've got the answer.

TRAVEL UNDERGROUND

Opening on January 9, 1863 – the world's first underground railway.

The steam trains of the Metropolitan Line will pull passengers in open carriages on the 4.8-kilometre (3-mile) journey from Paddington to the City in just 18 minutes (it takes 90 minutes by horse-drawn omnibus!)

* Some people say the trains will go so fast passengers will not be able to breathe. We guarantee this is not the case (we hope!).

Out and about
An Inside Guide to the Slums

You wouldn't want to visit a slum – so try reading our handy guide instead.

- **The poor** rent rooms in small terraced houses.
- **Up to 40 people** might be crammed into a single house.
- **The cheapest rooms** are at the back and the top of the house.
- **Many houses** have no running water and just a hole in the ground for a lavatory.
- **Crowded, dirty conditions** are breeding grounds for all kinds of bugs and diseases such as cholera.
- **Cheap houses** are built quickly and soon begin to crumble. No wonder people spend most of their time on the streets.

City **Tips:** ✔ Try the **suburbs**, where houses have **GARDENS**. ✔ Choose a good **rail or bus** route.

Welcome to **New York**

With hundreds of thousands of Europeans flooding into the city, buildings intended to house one family are divided up again and again. Their tall, narrow houses are mainly on the Lower East Side. They have no plumbing or proper ventilation, and have only very poor lighting.

What a **Pong!**

Even the greatest city in the world sometimes stinks! Remember the hot summer of 1858 in London? That was the year we called the Great Stink. The Thames River was like an open drain, full of human waste. Even the Houses of Parliament had to cover its windows with curtains to try and stop the stench from getting in.

We've built a huge sewer system now. It's one of the engineering marvels of the age. So with any luck nothing like the Great Stink can ever happen again.

Bad **Air**

If you visit London, beware of a 'pea-souper'. It's not something to eat. When the smoke from coal fires in factories and houses mingles with the air, it produces a thick yellowish-green smog. It's so thick that it really is almost like being in a soup. You can't see your own hand in front of you, let alone the end of the street.

One to **AVOID:** ✖ The slum at **FIVE POINTS** in Manhattan is one of the most dangerous places in America.

Getting AROUND

Steam power has changed the world. It's amazing to think that at the start of Victoria's reign we all travelled by horse-drawn carriage. Now we have railways and motor cars.

All at **Sea!**

age of the **Railway**

Since the first steam train carried passengers in 1825, railways have transformed our lives.

★ **Some trains now go as fast as 80 kilometres per hour (50 mph).** No-one has ever travelled as fast before!

★ **First class is the height of luxury,** with armchairs and food and drink; third class is like an unheated wooden box with open windows and hard bench seats.

★ **Railways** have led to a huge increase in the growth of places to live on the edges of cities, which have come to be known as 'suburbs'.

★ **In the United States**, the first transcontinental railway was completed in Utah in 1869.

★ **The coming of the railways** brought settlers to the American Midwest – and was the beginning of the end for Native American peoples.

For the millions of Europeans who have left their homes for the Americas during Victoria's reign, there is only one way to cross the ocean – by ship. Steamships have replaced sailing ships, cutting the journey time from 12 days to only 8.

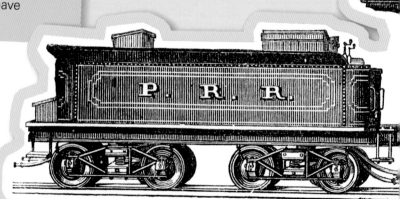

Ocean **Crossing:** ✔ **First class is very LUXURIOUS.** ✘ Steerage cabins are **CRAMPED** and airle

A **French** Import

You have to hand it to the French. It's thanks to them that London and New York have horse-drawn omnibuses. They were brought to London from Paris, and were soon a hit. They follow a set route and timetable. It costs more to sit inside than to sit on the upper deck.

Their maximum speed is 13 kilometres per hour (8 mph) – but they save us from walking miles!

High rider
Penny farthings had about 20 years of popularity.

Pedal Power

The bicycle has had a few false starts. The craziest was probably the penny farthing of the 1870s, with a huge wheel in front and a tiny one at the back (the penny and the farthing, like the old coins). The huge wheel means you can go very fast, but you have to have very good balance ... and a ladder for getting on and off!

Full steam ahead!

 Ships are getting **QUICKER all** the time. ✖ But there are still **DISASTERS** – even **STEAMSHIPS** can sink!

9

Our homes are OUR CASTLES

Providing a roof over his family's head is the job of every Victorian man. Everyone dreams of having their own home – and perhaps even a domestic servant or two?

Suburbia
Houses are all the same so they can be built quickly and cheaply.

* IDEAL HOMES! *
We far prefer the privacy of our own houses to apartments in the city.

Moving Out

The railways have opened up a whole new world for city dwellers. Now families can move out of the city centre to bigger houses because the father can easily travel to work in the city. Suburbs are spreading on the edges of all the biggest cities. The rows of terraced houses might all look the same and be furnished in the same way, but who cares? There's room at the top of the house for a servant while the family lives on the floors below. The kitchen is the servant's territory and is always in the basement. And there is usually a garden at the back.

What servants do YOU need?:  **BUTLER** – runs the entire household.

AN AMERICAN KITCHEN

Only the richest families in America have servants. Everyone else takes advantage of the latest gadgets and machines to save time and effort.

- A refrigerator keeps your milk and meat chilled and stops it from spoiling.
- An electric cooker lets you prepare food without having to light a fire in a stove.
- An electric iron speeds up ironing without needing to heat up the iron on a hotplate.
- A vacuum cleaner sucks up dust to clean carpets and rugs – no more beating by hand!

Learn from **Mrs B!**

★ *Confused about how to run your house?*

★ *Not sure how to instruct your servants?*

Get *Mrs Beeton's Book of Household Management* (1861). Recipes for favourite dishes. Tips on cleaning. Advice for when a child is sick.

★ *More than two million copies sold!*

Plumbed-In

With more homes having running water, soon everyone will have a bathroom. Usually, there's a water closet (or toilet) outside the house or in the cellar.

The Parlour

The heart of the house is the parlour, or living room. Check the latest magazines for tips on decoration. We think a room looks best when it's crowded with plants, birdcages, china, pictures and fire screens, as well as sofas and chairs. A piano will provide hours of entertainment. Curtains will help keep the room warm in winter and will keep the sun out in the summer.

✖ **FOOTMAN** – lets in visitors and waits at the table; an indulgence! ✔ **Cook** – makes sure you eat!

11

America RULES!

Welcome to NEW YORK!

Gateway City

Fancy a new life? Hundreds of thousands of Europeans are sailing across the Atlantic Ocean each year. From what we hear, North America has plenty of land to spare for everyone.

As the steamship sails past the Statue of Liberty, new arrivals can easily see how modern New York City looks. Skyscrapers loom on the horizon.

New arrivals come through Ellis Island, where their papers are checked and they have a medical. Most immigrants are poor. They live in slums where the housing might be worse than they had in Europe! Many decide to head west to discover the rest of the continent.

WANTED PIONEERS!

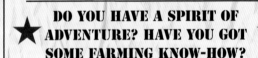

★ DO YOU HAVE A SPIRIT OF ADVENTURE? HAVE YOU GOT SOME FARMING KNOW-HOW? ★

Head west! There's a huge country out there, and we need settlers.

★

The Santa Fe or Union Railroad will get you from New York to California (on the West Coast) in only 13 days.

★

If that's too far, get off the train in the Midwest. There are small settlements everywhere that need more residents.

★

Since President Abraham Lincoln signed the Homestead Act in 1862, any settler who pays a small fee and follows some rules is entitled to 160 acres of public land. Stake a claim to your patch – and off you go!

Is **West Best?:** ✓ FREE LAND. ✗ Few stores. ✓ NO OVERCROWDING.

Wild West

Don't believe everything you hear! Cowboys drive huge herds of cattle to towns where they are put on railroad cars to be taken to the big cities. Some people think it's an adventurous life. In fact, it's very hard. Cowboys are usually extremely poor. They're not like the heroic figures as presented in Buffalo Bill's famous travelling shows!

A Hard Life

Life on the Frontier isn't easy. Here's our guide to dangers to avoid.

★ **Outlaws** There's not much law and order in some places, so gunfighters and robbers

★ **Range Bosses** Men who raise huge herds of animals bully homesteaders– because they want all the land for grazing.

★ **Loneliness** Remember, your nearest neighbour might be miles away. The West is a hard place for people who love a good chat!

★ **Climate** The summers are very hot but winters can be freezing. And watch out for tornadoes in the Midwest!

★ **Snakes, disease, hunger, poor soil, drought, insects…** We could go on!

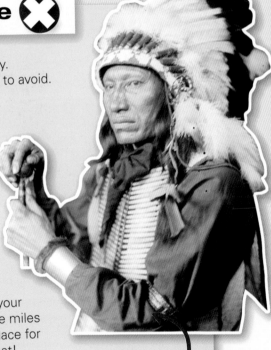

Friend or foe?
Treat Native Americans well – remember, they were here first!

Meet
A New American

Q. What's your name?
A. It was Francesco Grimaldi – but the immigration officer just changed it to Frank Grimes on my papers!

Q. How was the crossing?
A. Eight days being seasick! That was no fun.

Q. What are your first impressions of America?
A. I didn't like Ellis Island. The doctors turned away many people who had infectious diseases or even just bad eyesight. Others did not have the right papers. Families were being split up. No wonder they call it the Isle of Tears.

 ✗ Poor **schools.** ✔ **HEALTHY** lifestyle. ✗ No **NEIGHBOURS.** ✗ **NO ELECTRICITY.** ✗ Lots of **DANGER!**

Get the LOOK!

We Victorians are a sombre, sober and modest bunch when it comes to our dress. We've given up completely on the bright colours of the Georgian and Regency periods.

Fashion Rules for Men

★ Wear dark colours. They make you look more serious. Checks and stripes are out.

★ For work, stick to a suit of trousers, jacket and a waistcoat, and a white shirt.

★ For a change, try wearing a type of neck scarf called a cravat, instead of a tie.

★ Tweed is only ever to be worn in the countryside.

★ Knickerbockers are acceptable only for cycling, golfing or shooting.

Get ahead, get a HAT

hats, hats, hats

Everyone wears a hat. You can tell a lot about a man from his hat. Working men and boys wear cloth caps; middle-class men wear bowler hats to the office. The aristocracy wear top hats. For special occasions, the hats are made from grey silk but usually they are black. Ever since Prince Albert wore a straw hat, the straw boater has been the fashion statement for this summer.

Daring invention: ✔ **Amelia Bloomer** has invented 'BLOOMERS', like pyjama trousers for women.

> I wish I could loosen this corset for a minute!

Hoops
The New York Omnibus Company has raised its fares for 'ladies with hoops' because crinolines take up so much room.

fashion **Tips** for women

★ **Cover up!** We don't show any flesh apart from the hands and face. Dresses should have long sleeves and high necks, and should reach the floor.

The waist is back!
Squeeze your waist as small as possible with a corset. Corsets have bone ribs and laces to squeeze your figure – but they make if difficult to breathe!

★ **Try a crinoline!** This hooped frame holds your skirt out in a bell shape. But some crinolines have grown so wide that only three women can fit into a normal-sized room at the same time.

If the crinoline is
too inconvenient, gather your skirts behind you in a big bustle. Just make sure you can still sit down!

Stylewatch

Trendsetter

Queen Victoria flies the flag for Britain. She always wears clothes made here. She was one of the great beauties of Europe, and she set trends everywhere. Her delicate silver–white lace wedding dress was widely copied. After her beloved husband Albert died in 1861, she began wearing black as a sign that she was in mourning. Previously this was unusual, but now everyone wears black to show they are in mourning.

Blue Jeans

Could this be one of the most important fashion inventions of all? In 1873, Levi Strauss and Jacob Davis registered a patent to strengthen the seams of trousers with rivets. Their overalls and trousers are popular with miners. They are made from hard-wearing cloth called denim, for the cotton from France called 'serge de Nîmes'. Levi Strauss calls his clothes jeans. Who knows if they'll catch on?

Classic cut
The company that Levi Strauss founded is still going strong!

✔ They are **great for cycling.** ✘ People are **so outraged** that even Mrs Bloomer has **STOPPED** wearing them.

Food and Drink

We Victorians love to eat – and there's more variety of food now than ever before. (Of course, there are still many people who go hungry or eat very badly, too.)

STREET FOOD

For people without kitchens at home, buy hot meals from street vendors. Pies, pasties, muffins, potatoes and eels are always popular. The poor love oysters. They are so cheap!

A nice cup of tea

Tea is so popular that some servants even receive part of their wages in the form of tea leaves!

Party Tips

We often entertain in restaurants, but if you have friends to your home, here's how to make the occasion go with a swing.

1 ★ Try afternoon tea. This new meal has bread and butter, sandwiches, scones or small cakes, all washed down with lots of hot tea. Lovely!

2 ★ For dinner, it's so old-fashioned for everyone to have three main courses from a choice of up to 20. The food may look great but it will be cold by the time your guests have served themselves.

3 ★ Try eating less, and have dishes served to your guests by a footman or another servant.

4 ★ Everyone drinks wine, and fortified wines like brandy and port are popular as a drink at the end of the evening.

5 ★ After the meal, the men will want to smoke so the women should retire to chat in the drawing room.

Dos and **don'ts** with drinks: ✔ TEA – we drink it with nearly **every meal**.

STOP! Food Dangers

Be careful what you put in your mouth! Some food suppliers use poisonous tricks.

★ Bakers add alum and chalk to make their bread look whiter.

★ Manufacturers add copper salts to pickles to add colour – safer to make your own at home.

★ Cooks add poisonous arsenic to food to give it a more tangy taste.

Thank goodness for the Adulteration of Food, Drink and Drugs Act 1872. It stopped most dodgy dealers in their tracks.

Pickle jar
If your pickles are too bright, they might not be safe!

Gruel!

Don't be really poor. They get to eat potato parings and rotten vegetables. In the workhouse, the diet is potatoes, bread, gruel and a bit of cheese.

Invented in the U.S.A.

Doughnuts 1847
Chewing gum 1848
Canned baked
    beans 1875
Coca Cola 1886
Potato chips 1853

Frying tonight!

Have you tried the latest craze? No-one is sure who started it. Perhaps it was John Lees, who started selling fried potato and battered fish from a wooden hut in Mossley, Lancashire, in 1863. Or perhaps it was the Jewish immigrant, Joseph Malin, who opened a fried fish shop in London's East End in 1860. The debate rages on.

Classic British dish!

 Water – a source of disease such as **CHOLERA**. ✔ Beer – **cheap** and **NUTRITIOUS**! ✖ Gin – it's too **alcoholic**.

17

Keeping up *Appearances*

The days of men and women wearing so much make-up that they look like painted dolls have gone. Make-up is all about looking natural. For women, a natural healthy look is prized above all other looks.

If only the Prince of Wales would make me his PRINCESS!

Lily Langtry's beauty **Tips**

Actress Lily Langtry is the beauty of the age. She's certainly won the heart of the Prince of Wales, heir to the throne. Here are her best beauty tips.

★ **Make-up** should look natural, but pale skin with pink cheeks is the look every respectable lady wants.

★ **Never** go out in the sun – your skin will darken and burn.

★ **To keep your skin lily-white,** try a couple of drops of arsenic in your morning drink – but not too much, as it's a deadly poison.

★ **Use a firescreen** to protect your skin from the heat of the fire.

★ **Make eyes sparkle** with drops of belladonna – but be careful, it's another deadly poison.

★ **My trick** to keep cheeks looking rosy and healthy is to pinch them from time to time!

your guide to **Facial hair:** ✔ **MOUSTACHES** Goatee beard – just for art

Get the **Gibson Girl** look

At the end of the 19th century, every young American woman and girl wants to look like a Gibson Girl. The look is based on the illustrations by the artist Charles Dana Gibson. The Gibson Girl has her hair piled high on her head. Her athletic, glamorous look is the one that every modern girl wants to copy.

New look
At the end of the century, it's fashionable for women to show their arms.

Stylewatch

Curl it up!

Ladies, put your wigs away! Showing off your natural hair is in. Part it in the middle and wear it in coils above or behind each ear. Use a silk net to hold the coils in place. Artistic types might try wearing their hair long.

Sparkling in Black

Always a fashion leader, Queen Victoria has started another trend since the death of Prince Albert in 1861. She ditched all her jewels apart from Whitby black jet (named for the town it comes from). Now everyone wears black jet. Rings, brooches and bracelets are all the deepest black.

A Crimean Legacy

Beards and moustaches are all the rage today. The hairy look has been 'in' since British soldiers came home from the Crimean War in 1855. They grew big beards to keep their faces warm in the freezing Crimean winter and then liked them. The new look has caused a storm – because most women hate it. In the United States, General Ambrose Burnside has started a fashion for wearing exaggerated sideburns.

Ambrose Burnside gave his name to sideburns.

 Handlebar moustaches – use too much **WAX!** ✔ **Sideburns** – grow some muttonchop whiskers!

19

You can't get the STAFF

Working life has improved enormously during Victoria's reign, but there are still a lot of jobs you wouldn't want to do. An office job beats most of our jobs on offer this week.

JOB RATING
★★★ Top Job ★★ Bearable ★ Oh Dear!

Sewer hunters ★

Sewer hunting involves scraping the sides of the city sewers looking for any kind of valuables. Hunters sometimes find coins or pieces of lost jewellery. But there's always a danger of flash floods or of getting sick from being in contact with the sewage itself.

Freak Show Attraction ★

People who are born different from everyone else sometimes join a freak show. It's like a travelling circus where the public pay to stare at poor people like midgets and dwarves, people who are very fat or very thin and even conjoined twins. Other favourite attractions are strongmen, bearded ladies and women with tattoos.

The Tattooed Lady!

Tattoos are for sailors – not RESPECTABLE women!

Careers advice: ✖ Dredgers – fish **DEAD** bodies out of the river. ✔ Clerks – copy out **document**

Factory Hand ★★

Most people work in factories, like textile mills for making cloth. The factories never stop, and workers work up to 18 hours a day. The work is dirty, boring and dangerous. Machines can easily tear off a hand or arm – and there are no laws to protect workers. So take care!

Death trap
Few machines in factories have safety fences, so they're very dangerous.

Age Limit!
New laws in the 1830s and 1840s have stopped children under nine from having to work in factories.

Dear Mrs Batton,

Our son Jimmy is eight years old. We want him to work to earn some extra money. Which job would you recommend?

Augusta Pursepincher

Dear Mrs Pursepincher,
There's so much choice for a small boy who's willing to work hard. Consider one of these jobs:

- **Chimney sweep**
Small children climb up inside narrow chimneys to clean them.
- **Miner**
Children as young as four work in coal mines opening doors.
- **Factory cleaner**
Children can clean underneath machines without the machines having to be switched off.
- **Crossing sweep**
London's streets are so full of horse manure that there is always a job brushing a path for pedestrians.

I hope that helps,
Mrs Batton

Coal Miner ★

Coal powers factories, steamships and steam trains. Mining is a real family business. Children as young as four work as trappers, holding open underground doors for wagons to pass through. Older children and mums pull and push the wagons of coal. Dad and the strongest boys dig the coal out of the rock with pickaxes. But beware of mine collapses or gas explosions. We hear it will soon be illegal for children under 10 to work in the mines.

 Pickers – pick through **piles** of RUBBISH! Engine **drivers** – get to **DRIVE** trains! Teacher – well **respected**.

In our SPARE time

Although we Victorians work hard, many of us have more leisure time, too. With more money in our pockets, simple coffeehouses and taverns are 'old news'.

At the start of Victoria's reign, the word 'sport' described hunting, shooting or fishing. Now there are all sorts of new sports – and because factories close on Saturday afternoons, everyone has a chance to get involved. In Britain football, rugby and cricket have been given standard rules. In the United States, they have American football, baseball and basketball. Tennis and athletics are very popular worldwide. And since the invention of the safety bicycle in the 1880s there are hundreds of new cycling clubs everywhere.

Some **Victorian** hobbies: ✔ Stamp collecting. ✔ **PLANT** collecting. ✖ Collecting **SPIDERS**.

To the Sea
If you live in the North, head to Blackpool. From London, Brighton or Broadstairs are both an easy day trip.

I do **like** to be beside the **Seaside**

Everyone loves the seaside. Thanks to the railway, we can all get to the coast for a weekend or for one of the new 'bank holidays'.

★ **Try a walk along the seafront.** Take the promenade. This raised pavement will stop you getting sand in your boots. You'll also see and be seen by others.

★ **Hire a canvas deckchair and sit on the beach.**

★ **Give children buckets and spades** for building sand castles or collecting weird-looking animals from rock pools. Don't let them take them home!

★ **Try an ice cream** in an edible cornet.

★ **Punch and Judy** puppet shows always gather a crowd. But watch out for Mister Punch. There's a reason for his name!

A good **READ!**

These days nearly everyone can read. We have all sorts of choices: newspapers; 'penny-dreadfuls' for sensational stories of crime; and all kinds of novels and books. Public libraries have opened across Britain and the United States.

● **The Bible:** of course. It's the biggest-selling book ever.

● **Lewis Carroll's *Alice In Wonderland*** – a great children's story written by an Oxford professor. See if you can spot all the hidden mathematical references!

● **Many people** enjoy self-improvement books that teach them how to behave correctly or eat well.

● **Charles Dickens' stories about London continue to thrill.** Mr Dickens' books are published in magazines in monthly instalments. He loves to leave readers with a cliffhanger. Will young orphan Oliver ever find his mother?

We're all Consumers now

There has never been a better time to go shopping. The variety of goods on sale is amazing. And now our biggest cities have department stores that sell anything and almost everything!

Harrods in London was built in the 1890s.

Royal approval

The Queen and the royal family have granted more than 2,000 warrants. That means shops who supply the royal family can use the royal coat of arms. Having a royal warrant is prestigious. If a shop's goods are good enough for the queen, they must be good enough for the rest of us!

CHOICES, CHOICES!

We've seen them in Paris, London, New York and Chicago. Since the 1850s, stores with many separate departments are the place to shop. Fixed prices are displayed for all goods and there are plenty of assistants to help. Better still, unlike your local shop, you can look around and leave without buying anything. In London, visit Dickens and Jones or Harrods. In New York, Macy's and Lord and Taylor's are worth a visit. They stock everything: clothing, household goods, toys – even sports equipment.

Shop by **catalogue:** ✓ Order **ANYTHING** you want by POST. ✓ Wide **RANGE** of choice

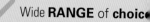

Let's **Co-operate**

The Rochdale Equitable Pioneers Society in Lancashire has come up with a way of shopping that has gained worldwide attention. The society buys in bulk, so it gets good prices. Then it sells on the groceries loose to its members. That way shoppers only buy what they need – and get the same low price, too. They call the arrangement a co-operative. It looks as if it could catch on everywhere.

Starving hungry
The Victorian poor got money by begging – or stealing!

A woman's **job**

In the high street, you'll see that women do nearly all the shopping. But shopping can be a challenge. In local shops the goods are kept behind the counter so you can't see them. Some shopkeepers decide to charge more if their customers look rich.

Dear Mrs Batton,

I've been selling fish in the streets from my barrow for years. There used to be loads of us selling food. But now no-one buys from us.

Yours sincerely,

John Fish, Fish's Fish

Dear John Fish,
Get with the times! New shops are opening everywhere. They're cleaner – and quieter – than the streets. The prices are all fixed, and they have more choice. Barrows are on their way out. Time to find another job!
Must run – off to the grocer's.
Yours,
Mrs. Batton

Get in the Festive Spirit!

let's **decorate** the **tree!**

It's hard to imagine but at the start of the 19th century nobody celebrated Christmas. It took our very own German-born Prince Albert to show us what fun we can have if we allow ourselves to!

When Prince Albert moved to England, he brought all his German traditions with him. In 1841 he and Queen Victor decorated a fir tree at Windsor Castle with lighted candles, sweets, fruit, homemade decorations and small gifts. Now everyone wants a Christmas tree. There's nothing prettier than a tre glowing with candles or a winter's afternoon. Indeed, the *Illustrate Daily News* showed the royal family with their tree in the Christmas 1848 issue.

Deck the HALLS!

Dear Mrs Beeton,

How do I cook a pudding for Christmas?

Yours sincerely,
Thumbelina Pecksniff

Dear Thumbelina,
Put raisins, currants, mixed peel, suet, eggs and brandy in a large bowl. Let the whole family have a turn stirring the pudding. Add some coins for luck. Tie the mixture in a cloth and boil it for six hours. To serve, cover the pudding with brandy and then set it alight.

Yours, Mrs Beeton

A Victorian **CHRISTMAS:** ✔ Presents. ✔ **GREETINGS** cards. ✔ **TREE.** ✔ **PUDDING.**

Christmas Greetings

Can you believe the first Christmas card cost a day's wages? The hand-made card had an illustration of a family having dinner and a Christmas message. But you don't need to pay so much. Make your own cards (the royal family do) or buy cheaper printed cards. In 1880, Britons sent 1.5 million Christmas Cards!

White ideal
Cards include lovely symbols like snow and holly.

A Merry Christmas.

Gifts Galore!

We used to exchange gifts at New Year but now it's Christmas Day. (Prince Albert and Queen Victoria exchange gifts on Christmas Eve because that's the tradition in Germany.) The British also follow the American idea of a Christmas stocking. Hang up a stocking over the fireplace and fill it with gifts and an orange.

Holidays

In Great Britain the holiday includes December 26 as well as Christmas Day. Boxing Day is when people pack up their old clothes to give them away to the poor. It's also a day off for the servants.

A CHRISTMAS CAROL!

Some people think that our favourite novelist, Charles Dickens, invented Christmas. But that's not true, although his story about Scrooge, *A Christmas Carol*, is a great moral tale about the meaning of Christmas. Christmas is about giving, after all, isn't it?

Read all about it!

Murder in the East End!

We Victorians read loads of newspapers and magazines. Scandals, murders, adventure: many people have become celebrities even though we wouldn't want to meet some of them!

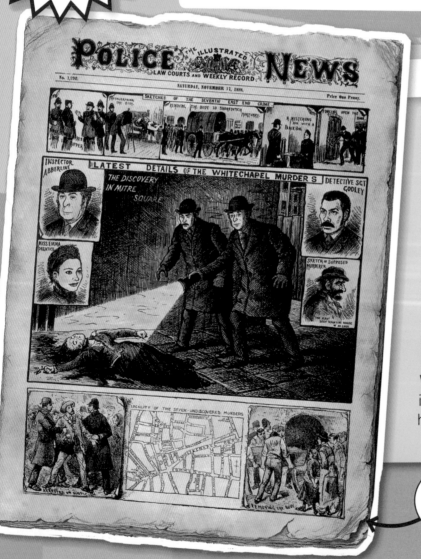

Jack the **Ripper**

He (or might he be a she?) is definitely the most famous murderer of our age. Jack terrorised London's East End during 1888. His eight victims were chopped up in a gruesome way. He cut up his victims so cleanly, some people have said he must be a surgeon. Others even suggest he might be a member of the royal family. What we do know is that he isn't called Jack – and that he is still on the loose.

Police News
Newspapers carried sensational illustrations of the murder scenes.

Celebrities to meet or not: ✔ Queen Victoria . ✔ Lily Langtry.

"Doctor **Livingstone,** I presume?"

When the Scottish missionary David Livingstone went missing in Africa in 1865, a newspaper sent Henry Stanley to find him. Nothing had been heard of Livingstone for four years; most people thought he was dead. But Stanley found him two years later, in 1871. (There is no happy ending – Livingstone died in Africa in 1873. But his dedication to spreading his faith has inspired us for years.)

Your **money** or your **life!**

The outlaw Jesse James raided banks and trains. But Jesse was no Robin Hood – he did not rob to help the poor, just to help himself! So he wasn't really a hero. No-one was surprised when one of his gang shot him in 1882 in order to claim the $5,000 reward!

African-American **Pioneer**

After Barney Ford escaped from slavery in Virginia, he sailed to Nicaragua in Central America, where he ran a hotel. He moved to Colorado and made a fortune as a miner – but lost it all to a crooked lawyer. So Ford opened another hotel and dealt in property until he became the richest man in town – again!

Two fortunes isn't bad for a former slave, if you ask me!

THE JERSEY LILY

What woman hasn't wished she was Lily Langtry, with her good looks? The heir to the English throne, the Prince of Wales, is a great admirer of the actress from Jersey. Lily is so popular in the United States that she has become a U.S. citizen.

Glossary

barrow A wheeled cart for selling goods in the street.

butler The male servant in charge of running a household.

cholera A deadly disease that is transmitted by infected water.

colonies Overseas territories governed by the same country.

corset A wide, beltlike garment that women (and some men) use to squeeze in their waists.

footman A servant who welcomes visitors and serves at the table.

Frontier The name given to the thinly settled regions of the Midwest in the United States.

instalment A section of a book or story that is published in parts.

jet A hard black stone that can be polished to a shine.

knickerbockers Loose fitting trousers that are gathered at the knee.

mourning A period after someone's death when people wear dark clothes and avoid enjoyment.

omnibus An early form of public transport using two-deck carriages.

parlour The main living room of a Victorian home.

penny farthing A bicycle with a huge front wheel and a small back wheel.

prudish Describes someone who is easily offended.

safety bicycle A bicycle with wheels of equal sizes.

slum An area of poor, overcrowded housing with few comforts.

smog A thick mist formed by a mixture of fog and smoke.

suburbia A residential area on the edge of a city.

On the web

www.bbc.co.uk/schools/primaryhistory/victorian_britain/
BBC schools site all about the Victorians and their lives.

http://www.bbc.co.uk/history/british/victorians/
Another BBC site, with more information about the Victorians.

http://www.bl.uk/victorian-britain
A guide from the British Library to the Victorians and their times.

Books

Barber, Nicola. *School* (Victorian Life). Wayland Books, 2012.

Bingham, Jane. *Victorians* (Explore!). Wayland Books, 2014.

Brocklehurst, Ruth. *Victorians* (Usborne History of Britain). Usborne Publishing Ltd., 2008.

Cooper, Alison. *The Victorians* (History Relived). Wayland Books, 2012.

Deary, Terry. *The Vile Victorians* (Horrible Histories). Scholastic, 2007.

Kramer, Ann. *Victorians* (Eyewitness). Dorling Kindersley, 2011.

Macdonald, Fiona. *Avoid Being a Victorian Servant!* (The Danger Zone). Book House, 2005.

Malam, John. *Avoid Being a Victorian Mill Worker!* (The Danger Zone). Book House, 2008.

Triggs, Terry D. *Victorians* (Primary History). Collins, 2012.

Powell, Jillian. *Victorian Times* (Craft Box). Wayland Books, 2013.

Index

A
African Americans 29
Albert, Prince 4, 14, 15, 19, 26

B
beauty 18–19
Beeton, Isabella 11
bicycle 9
British empire 4, 5
Buffalo Bill 13
Burnside, Ambrose 19

C
Carroll, Lewis 23
celebrities 28–29
Christmas 26–27
A Christmas Carol 27
cities 6–7, 9, 12, 28
co-operative movement 25
cowboys 13
Crimean War 19
crinoline 15

D
department stores 24
Dickens, Charles 23, 27

F
factories 21
fashion 14–15
food and drink 16–17
Ford, Barney 29
freak shows 20
Frontier, American 13

G
Gibson Girl 19

H
hairstyles 19
hats 14
homes 10–11

IJ
immigration 12, 13
Jack the Ripper 28
James, Jesse 29
jeans 15
jobs 20–21

K
kitchens 11, 16

L
Langtry, Lily 18, 29
Levi Strauss, Claude 15
Livingstone, David 29
London 6, 7, 9, 28

M
make-up 18–19
mining 21

N
New York 7, 12
newspapers 23, 28

P
pastimes 22–23

R
railways 4, 8, 12
reading 23
royal warrants 24

S
seaside holidays 23
shopping 24–25
slums 6
sports 22
Stanley, Henry M. 29
suburbs 10

T
transport 8–9

U
underground railway 6
United States 7, 8, 12–13, 29

V
Victoria, Queen 4, 5, 15, 17, 19, 24

W
Wild West 13
women's roles 24